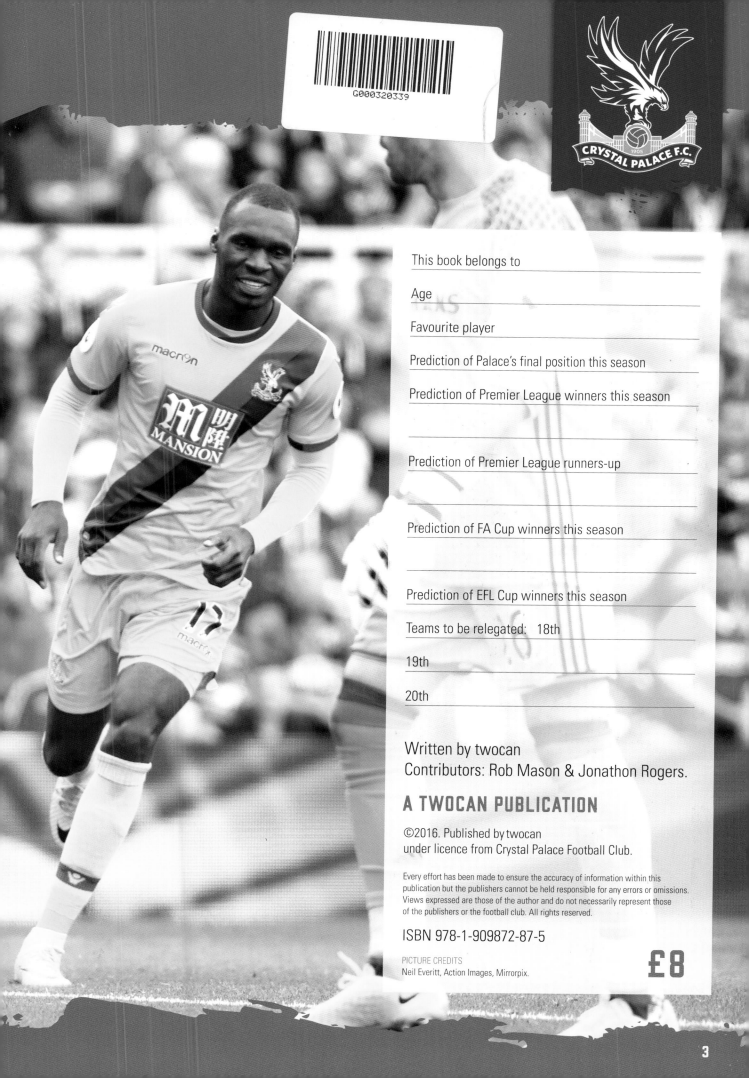

CRYSTAL PALACE F.C.
1905

This book belongs to

Age

Favourite player

Prediction of Palace's final position this season

Prediction of Premier League winners this season

Prediction of Premier League runners-up

Prediction of FA Cup winners this season

Prediction of EFL Cup winners this season

Teams to be relegated: 18th

19th

20th

Written by twocan
Contributors: Rob Mason & Jonathon Rogers.

A TWOCAN PUBLICATION

©2016. Published by twocan
under licence from Crystal Palace Football Club.

ISBN 978-1-909872-87-5

PICTURE CREDITS
Neil Everitt, Action Images, Mirrorpix.

£8

CONTENTS

JULIAN SPERONI | 01

POSITION: Goalkeeper NATIONALITY: Argentinian DOB: 18.05.1979

DID YOU KNOW? Shot-stopper Julian is a legend at Selhurst Park having been with the club for over a decade and he has won a record four Player of the Year awards.

JOEL WARD | 02

POSITION: Defender NATIONALITY: English DOB: 29.10.1989

DID YOU KNOW? Since arriving at Selhurst Park in 2012, Joel has showed his versatility and commitment by excelling in a variety of positions including left-back and central midfield.

MATHIEU FLAMINI | 04

POSITION: Midfielder **NATIONALITY:** French **DOB:** 07.03.1984

DID YOU KNOW? After the Eagles swooped to sign free-agent Mathieu in September 2016, the Frenchman made his debut three days later in the 2-1 win against 'Boro at the Riverside.

JAMES TOMKINS | 05

POSITION: Defender **NATIONALITY:** English **DOB:** 29.03.1989

DID YOU KNOW? New signing James has represented his country at all levels from Under-15s up to England Under-21s and was part of Team GB's Olympic squad in 2012.

SCOTT DANN | 06

POSITION: Defender NATIONALITY: English DOB: 14.02.1987

DID YOU KNOW? Named the club's Player of the Year for 2014/15 in his first full season, new club captain Scott, followed up by winning the Player's Player of the Year award for 2015/16.

YOHAN CABAYE | 07

POSITION: Midfielder NATIONALITY: French DOB: 14.01.1986

DID YOU KNOW? Yohan, who played 40 times in all competitions and netted six times in his debut season with the Eagles, was part of the French squad that came so close to winning Euro 2016.

LOIC REMY | 08

POSITION: Striker **NATIONALITY:** French **DOB:** 02.01.1987

DID YOU KNOW? French international Loic made the switch from the west of the capital to south in the summer, signing for the Eagles on a season-long loan from Chelsea.

FRAIZER CAMPBELL | 09

POSITION: Striker **NATIONALITY:** English **DOB:** 13.09.1987

DID YOU KNOW? Fraizer, who began his career at Manchester United progressing through the Red Devils' academy, has represented England from Under-16 level right up to full international.

ANDROS TOWNSEND | 10

POSITION: Midfielder NATIONALITY: English DOB: 16.07.1991

DID YOU KNOW? The England winger, who rose through the ranks at Spurs, was the first Eagles summer signing of 2016, arrived from Newcastle for a fee of £13 million.

WILFRIED ZAHA | 11

POSITION: Midfielder NATIONALITY: English DOB: 10.11.1992

DID YOU KNOW? Since returning from Man Utd in January 2015, Wilfried's superb displays have helped the club reach the FA Cup final and earned him the Player of the Season award for 2015/16.

WAYNE HENNESSEY | 13

POSITION: Goalkeeper **NATIONALITY:** Welsh **DOB:** 24.01.1987

DID YOU KNOW? Wayne, who has been a regular for Wales since his debut in 2007, now has more the 50 caps for his country and was part of the Red Dragons' successful Euro 2016 campaign.

CHUNG-YONG LEE | 14

POSITION: Midfielder **NATIONALITY:** South Korean **DOB:** 02.07.1988

DID YOU KNOW? Lee has more than 70 caps to his name and is a huge star in his homeland. He has represented his country in two World Cups, scoring twice in the 2010 competition.

JONATHAN BENTEKE | 15

POSITION: Striker **NATIONALITY:** Belgian **DOB:** 28.04.1995

DID YOU KNOW? Jonathan, who is the brother of Christian, made his Eagles debut in the 2-1 win against 'Boro at the Riverside, when he came on as a late substitute for Benteke senior.

JOE LEDLEY | 16

POSITION: Midfielder **NATIONALITY:** Welsh **DOB:** 23.01.1987

DID YOU KNOW? Joe has over 50 caps for his country and was part of Chris Coleman's Euro 2016 squad despite fracturing his fibula only six weeks before the competition began.

SQUAD 2016/17

CHRISTIAN BENTEKE | 17

POSITION: Striker NATIONALITY: Belgian DOB: 03.12.1990

DID YOU KNOW? Christian, Palace's club record transfer from Liverpool, was part of Belgium's Euro 2016 squad, playing twice in the wins over the Republic of Ireland and Sweden.

JAMES MCARTHUR | 18

POSITION: Midfielder NATIONALITY: Scottish DOB: 07.10.1987

DID YOU KNOW? James, who has been capped more than 20 times by Scotland, played the full game as Wigan Athletic shocked Manchester City to lift the 2013 FA Cup.

ZEKI FRYERS | 19

POSITION: Defender NATIONALITY: English DOB: 09.09.1992

DID YOU KNOW? Zeki is a product of the Man Utd academy, and after making his Red Devils debut in the League Cup in 2011, he went on to appear in the Champions League under Sir Alex Ferguson.

CONNOR WICKHAM | 21

POSITION: Striker NATIONALITY: English DOB: 31.03.1993

DID YOU KNOW? Connor made his pro-debut aged just 16 years and 11 days to became the Tractor Boys' youngest-ever player. He has also played 17 times for England Under-21s, scoring six times.

JORDON MUTCH | 22

POSITION: Midfielder NATIONALITY: English DOB: 02.12.1991

DID YOU KNOW? Jordon, who began his career with Birmingham City, arrived in January 2015 as Alan Pardew's second signing as Palace manager when arriving from QPR.

PAPE SOUARE | 23

POSITION: Defender NATIONALITY: Senegalese DOB: 06.06.1990

DID YOU KNOW? Pape, a product of Lille's academy, has experience of Champions League and Europa League football with the French side. He is a full international and also played in the 2012 Olympics.

BAKARY SAKO | 26

POSITION: Midfielder **NATIONALITY:** Malian **DOB:** 26.04.1988

DID YOU KNOW? After joining from Wolves on the eve of the 2015/16 season, Bakary made an instant impact by netting a late winner against Aston Villa on his debut for the Eagles.

DAMIEN DELANEY | 27

POSITION: Defender **NATIONALITY:** Irish **DOB:** 20.07.1981

DID YOU KNOW? Republic of Ireland international Damien is a firm fans' favourite and has been a regular in the Eagles' defence since their promotion-winning campaign of 2012/13.

STEVE MANDANDA | 30

POSITION: Goalkeeper **NATIONALITY:** French **DOB:** 28.03.1985

DID YOU KNOW? Steve signed from Marseille in June 2016, while he was on duty with the French Euro 2016 squad. Last season he was named Ligue 1 Goalkeeper of the Year for the fourth time.

MARTIN KELLY | 34

POSITION: Defender NATIONALITY: English DOB: 27.04.1990

DID YOU KNOW? After arriving from Liverpool, Martin netted his first Palace goal against Spurs to take the Eagles into the FA Cup quarter-finals and eventually the 2016 final.

LUKE DREHER | 35

POSITION: Midfielder NATIONALITY: English DOB: 27.11.1998

DID YOU KNOW? Luke, the club's Academy Player of the Year, got his first taste of first-team action earlier this season, coming on as a second-half substitute in a friendly at Fulham.

JASON PUNCHEON | 42

POSITION: Midfielder NATIONALITY: English DOB: 26.06.1986

DID YOU KNOW? Jason grew up a stone's throw away from Selhurst Park and has now become one of his boyhood club's key players with over 100 appearances for the Eagles under his belt.

YOHAN CABAYE 7

Can you spot the season from these five clues?

SPOT THE SEASON

Palace made Nigel Martyn the first million pound goalkeeper when he signed from Bristol Rovers

Mark Bright top-scored with 17 goals (12 league and 5 cup) and was named Player of the Year

Crystal Palace survived their first season back in the top flight, finishing in 15th place

Alan Pardew celebrates his extra-time winner in the 4-3 FA Cup win over Liverpool

Steve Coppell leads out the team for the FA Cup final

ANSWER ON PAGE 62

SKILLS: THE CRUYFF TURN

1 Draw back your foot as if you are going to kick the ball

2 Instead of following through, stop your foot over the ball...

...and push it back behind your other leg while starting to turn your body. **3**

4 Finish turning through 180° and head in the opposite direction.

Your unsuspecting opponent will be left standing wondering what just happened! **5**

Johan Cruyff debuted his signature dummy at the 1974 FIFA World Cup. The trick is a brilliant manoeuvre to fool your opponent and change direction.

JASON PUNCHEON

V NORWICH CITY – 9TH APRIL 2016

GOAL OF THE SEASON

Arguably the most important goal of Palace's season was swept home by the Eagles winger to provide relief to him and the 25,000 in attendance at Selhurst.

After Chung-yong Lee's wonderstrike had beaten Stoke City in December, Alan Pardew's side had to wait over three months and 16 games to finally taste that winning feeling once again, and a turgid, nervy encounter against the Canaries - then attempting to suck the Eagles into the battle for the drop - saw just one moment of quality, which came from the left boot of Puncheon.

Desperate to score his first of the season, the boyhood Palace fan found himself drifting with the ball out to the right touchline, and so passed it off to Scott Dann. The centre-back then found Joel Ward, which allowed Puncheon the chance to overlap past the right-back and take control of the situation just outside the Norwich box.

His first touch saw him push the ball into the perfect place to get a shot away, and he promptly pulled the trigger and fired around Sebastien Bassong just out the reach of John Ruddy. The ball caressed the side-netting before settling in the goal, allowing an emotional Puncheon and his teammates to celebrate enthusiastically as over three months' worth of frustration was released.

Can you find the eight difference between these two action shots

ANSWERS ON PAGE 62

22

EAGLES Rule!

The 71st minute of the friendly at Fulham earlier this season was a moment that Luke Dreher will never forget.

As he was taking in the surroundings, he got the call from Alan Pardew to strip off and prepare himself for his first taste of life in the Palace first-team.

It was a huge step for the 17-year-old who a year ago was still with the Eagles' Under-18s, but a brilliant 12 months has seen him establish himself in the development side, win the club's Academy Player of the Year award, named on the bench for the Premier League game at Manchester United and make his full Palace bow.

The Cottagers may have won the game 3-1 but Dreher impressed during his time on the pitch playing alongside Mile Jedinak and Jonny Williams just in front of the back four, and the teenager made the pass of the match to set up Keshi Anderson's goal which capped a brilliant day for the academy product.

After a second taste of first-team action three days later at Bromley, Dreher has returned to the development squad, and after making big advances last season he knows that more of the same will see appearances at grounds like Craven Cottage become a much more regular occurrence.

YOUNG GUN
LUKE
DREHER

ANDROS 10
TOWNSEND

CRYSTAL PALACE F.C.

A — Captained Arsenal to the European Cup Winners' Cup win in 1994

B — Hull City played their home game here before moving to the KC Stadium

C — Crystal Palace's all-time top appearance maker

D — He scored two goals in Swansea's 5-0 League Cup final win over Bradford in 2013

E — He spent a successful seven-year spell at Chelsea

F — Man City retired squad number 23 in memory of this player

G — Burnley's top scorer last season

The answer to each clue begins with the corresponding letter of the alphabet

H — Led Bournemouth to promotion to the Premier League in 2014/15

I — Meaning of the latin phrase 'Consectatio Excellentiae' on SAFC's crest

J — Honorary life president of Watford FC

K — Manchester City's Belgian captain

L — Man Utd have won the FA Cup 12 times, this man scored the winner in the 2016 final

M — Manager of Boro when they won the League Cup in 2004

ANSWERS ON PAGE 62

GARETH SOUTHGATE

A classy and versatile player, Southgate went on to win 57 England caps and manage England Under-21s. A stylish skipper for Palace, Gareth was always a leader.

NIGEL MARTYN

Capped three times by England while with Palace, Martyn cost £1m in 1989 and was sold for over £2m almost seven years later after 349 appearances, including the 1990 FA Cup final.

JIM CANNON

Palace's record appearance maker, Cannon played 660 times for the club, all but four of them starts. Player of the Year in 1978, he is the only post-war player to have two testimonials at the club. He was also Player of the Year in 1985 and 1987.

PAUL HINSHELWOOD

Player of the Year in 1980 and 1981, Paul Hinshelwood was a real team player who made 319 appearances for the club, becoming an effective right back after starting as a striker.

WILFRIED ZAHA

A fantastically tricky winger who developed through the Palace youth system to become an England international. After over 100 games as an Eagle, a big money move took Zaha to Manchester United but he found his best form after returning to Selhurst Park

KENNY SANSOM

An ever-present promotion winner in 1977 and '79, Sansom was Player of the Year in both campaigns, also captaining the FA Youth Cup winning side in the first of those. He went on to win 86 England caps, the first nine of them with Palace.

YANNICK BOLASIE

117 goals in 277 games, Wrighty scored twice in the 1990 FA Cup final having top scored in the promotion season a year before when he was Player of the Year. He won the first four of his 33 England caps while with Palace.

IAN WRIGHT

STEVE KEMBER

Croydon-born creator who was ever present in the team who won a first promotion to the top flight in 1969. Leaving in 1971 Steve returned in 1978, helped win the Second Division in 1979 and he twice permanently managed the club (4 times including caretaker).

TEAM

YOHAN CABAYE

Signed from PSG by Alan Pardew for whom Cabaye had excelled at Newcastle, this brilliant France international came to Palace in the summer of 2015 and immediately showed his class with a debut goal against Norwich.

PETER SIMPSON

The club's all time record goal-scorer, the Scot scored 165 times in 195 games, including 19 hat-tricks, having attracted interest playing against Palace in the FA Cup for Kettering in 1928. In 1930/31 he set a season scoring record of 46 league goals.

Signed from Bristol City in 2012 this super speedy forward is a DR Congo international who became the first Palace player to produce a Premier League hat-trick - and it took him just 11 minutes in a game at Sunderland in 2015.

13

WAYNE
HENNESSEY

Do you know where every Premier League team play their home games? Fill in the missing words and find all the grounds in the grid!

A	I	L	T	S	T	N	M	U	I	D	A	T	S	Y	T	I	L	A	T	I	V
H	N	S	V	I	C	A	R	A	G	E	R	O	A	D	J	Q	J	Z	K	A	O
F	L	F	D	U	E	K	R	A	P	N	O	S	I	D	O	O	G	R	C	L	W
R	M	D	I	A	M	E	G	D	I	R	B	D	R	O	F	M	A	T	S	N	H
I	U	H	M	E	J	F	B	J	T	K	S	E	B	I	Z	P	K	G	C	P	I
V	I	C	U	Y	L	N	G	D	R	O	F	F	A	R	T	D	L	O	K	Y	T
E	D	R	I	O	R	D	M	U	I	D	A	T	S	S	E	T	A	R	I	M	E
R	A	S	D	E	A	L	X	V	D	R	O	I	R	3	6	5	U	A	K	E	H
S	T	M	A	R	Y	S	S	T	A	D	I	U	M	K	D	F	B	N	N	R	A
I	S	G	T	H	M	E	U	P	T	M	H	G	L	U	C	P	Q	I	O	W	R
D	5	X	S	I	A	O	J	F	G	L	A	H	Y	O	I	S	Y	O	R	3	T
E	6	F	Y	A	E	S	M	W	E	E	G	V	W	H	P	D	M	T	B	5	L
S	3	E	T	I	H	A	D	S	T	A	D	I	U	M	K	F	A	P	I	6	A
T	T	C	R	C	O	R	V	Q	W	X	L	D	B	Z	R	H	I	T	A	M	N
A	E	H	E	V	O	T	H	G	I	L	F	O	M	U	I	D	A	T	S	L	E
D	B	W	B	F	Q	E	P	S	N	R	O	H	T	W	A	H	E	H	T	C	P
I	M	D	I	N	K	N	B	5	6	3	T	M	U	S	F	E	N	B	A	G	K
U	P	O	L	H	L	O	N	D	O	N	S	T	A	D	I	U	M	R	G	J	W
M	V	S	A	O	R	M	U	I	D	A	T	S	R	E	W	O	P	G	N	I	K

Team	Ground	Team	Ground	Team	Ground
Arsenal	_____ Stadium	**Leicester**	King _____ Stadium	**Sunderland**	Stadium of _____
Bournemouth	_____ Stadium	**Liverpool**	_____	**Swansea**	_____ Stadium
Burnley	____ Moor	**Man City**	_____ Stadium	**Tottenham**	_____ Hart ____
Chelsea	_____ Bridge	**Man United**	Old _____	**Watford**	_____ Road
Crystal Palace	_____ Park	**Middlesbrough**	_____ Stadium	**West Brom**	The _____
Everton	_____ Park	**Southampton**	St _____'_ Stadium	**West Ham**	_____ Stadium
Hull	KC _____	**Stoke**	_____ Stadium		

ARSENAL
LUCAS PEREZ

Signed from Deportivo La Coruna for a reported £17m just before the closure of the transfer window, 'Lucas' is a good fit for the Gunners. A player who looks to play 'one-two's' in and around the box the 28-year-old has played in Ukraine and Greece as well as Spain. Barcelona and Atletico Madrid were amongst his victims as he struck 18 times in 37 games last season, the best of his career so far.

BURNLEY
ANDRE GRAY

Having fired Burnley back into the Premier League in his first season at Turf Moor, 25-year-old Gray showed he intended to carry on in fine style in the Premier League with an early season goal in a sensational win over Liverpool. Wolverhampton born Andre came to the Clarets via Brentford who he'd joined after his goals brought Luton Town back into the Football League.

BOURNEMOUTH
CALLUM WILSON

Speed merchant Wilson made his name with his hometown team Coventry, costing the Cherries £3m in 2014. Having helped them into the Premier League he hit an early season hat-trick against West Ham but then picked up an injury which ruined his season. This time round he is hoping to show his Bourne supremacy.

CHELSEA
MICHY BATSHUAYI

Antonio Conte made Michy his first signing for the Blues, splashing out £33m on the young Belgium international. Strong and quick, Batshuayi could be Stamford Bridge's new Didier Drogba and like Drogba lists Marseille as one of his previous clubs. He also impressed with Standard Liege and is excellent at linking up play as well as putting the ball into the back of the net.

CRYSTAL PALACE
CHRISTIAN BENTEKE

Crystal Palace invested a club record £27m in Belgium striker Christian Benteke in the summer. The Eagles have a top class forward in Benteke who after beginning in Belgian footba scored 49 goals in 101 games for Ast Villa before a £32.5m move to Liverpo where he netted 10 times in 42 games

WATCH OUT FOR THESE DANGERMEN.

EVERTON
ROMELU LUKAKU

Still only 23, Lukaku is a powerhouse striker and probably the nearest thing in the game to his boyhood hero Didier Drogba. Romelu emulated his idol by making Chelsea his first English club. A debutant with Anderlecht when he had just turned 16, he excelled on loan from Chelsea to West Brom and subsequently moved to Everton, the Toffees making him their record signing at £28m. For Belgium he had scored 14 goals in 49 games at the start of this season.

LIVERPOOL
SADIO MANE

The scorer of the quickest hat-trick in Premier League history when he took just two minutes 56 seconds to net three times for Southampton against Aston Villa in 2015! The Senegal international speed merchant cost Liverpool £34m last summer, shortly after he'd scored twice against them, quickly followed by a hat-trick against Manchester City.

HULL CITY
DIEUMERCI MBOKANI

Signed just as the transfer window closed in the summer on loan from Dynamo Kiev, Mbokani came to Hull with experience of the Premier League having scored seven times on loan to Norwich last season. The 31-year-old DR Congo international has played in five countries and won six league titles and many cups.

LEICESTER CITY
JAMIE VARDY

Jamie Vardy is the reigning Footballer of the Year and Premier League Player of the Year. His hard work and dedication has seen him rise from non-league football to the dizzy heights of the Premier League. Last season he helped fire Leicester City to the top of the table and himself into the England team.

MANCHESTER CITY
SERGIO AGUERO

As dangerous as any dangerman in the Premier League 'Kun' Aguero is simply a goal machine. He's fired City to two Premier League titles and two League Cups and started this season with six goals in his first three games including a Champions League hat-trick. Last season his haul included a hat-trick against Chelsea and five goals in a blistering 20 minute spell against relegation bound Newcastle.

DANGER MEN

MANCHESTER UNITED
ZLATAN IBRAHIMOVIC

There are many stars in the Premier League and Zlatan Ibrahimovic is as big as any of them. The Super-Swede has finally arrived in English football this season after playing in the Netherlands, Italy, Spain and France as well as his own country. He has won the league title in 12 of his last 13 seasons and had scored 392 goals in 677 games at the start of this season.

SOUTHAMPTON
SOFIANE BOUFAL

Southampton broke their transfer record to bring in 22-year-old Morocco international attacking midfielder Sofiane Boufal shortly before the summer transfer window closed. Boufal began his career with Angers and came to the fore last season with Lille where he played in the final of the French League Cup against PSG a week after scoring a brilliant hat-trick against Ajaccio.

SUNDERLAND
JERMAIN DEFOE

Harry Kane and Jamie Vardy were the only English players to score more Premier League goals than Defoe last season. Jermain's tally of 15 included a hat-trick at Swansea when he claimed his second match ball of the campaign having also scored three in a League Cup tie with Exeter. At the start of this season Jermain was the last player to score a hat-trick for England and he will be looking for a return to the international fold now th his ex-Sunderland manager Sam Allardyce has taken over the national side.

MIDDLESBROUGH
ALVARO NEGREDO

A debut goal on the opening day of the season is likely to be the first of many for the man who, when at Manchester City, bagged hat-tricks in the Champions League and the semi-final of the League Cup. In between his spells in England, Negredo played for Valencia, a team he once scored four goals in a game against for Sevilla.

STOKE CITY
XHERDAN SHAQIRI

Swiss international who acrobatically scored one of the most spectacular goals at Euro 16 against Poland. Having won three league titles and a cup at the start of his career with FC Basel in Switzerland, he moved on to Bayern Munich with whom he won the Champions League in 2013, as well as the European Super Cup, the World Club Cup and two Bundesliga titles before moving on to another continental giant in Inter Milan before coming to Stoke.

WATCH OUT FOR THESE DANGERMEN

SWANSEA CITY
BORJA BASTON

Swansea spent £15.5m in August to bring in Spanish striker Borja Baston. Last season he ripped up la Liga with 18 goals in 29 starts and seven sub appearances with Eibar, including a goal away to Barcelona. In 2009 Baston won the Golden Boot by scoring five goals at the U17 World Cup and now he'll look to fulfil his potential in the Prem.

WEST BROMWICH ALBION
SALOMON RONDON

After taking time to get used to life in the Premier League, Venezuela international Salomon Rondon really looked to be getting to grips with the demands of English football by the end of his first season. Having come to Europe as a teenager in 2008 when he moved to Las Palmas his ability as a dangerman has since seen Malaga break their club record for him with Rubin Kazan investing £10m, Zenit St Petersburg a whopping £15.8m and West Brom a record £12m!

WATFORD
ODION IGHALO

Famed for his 'picture-goals' Odion has been with the Hornets since 2014. He scored 20 goals in his first season as Watford won promotion and scored 16 (plus a couple in the cups) in his first season in the Premier League when he won the League's Player of the Month award in December 2015. A Nigerian international, Ighalo played in Nigeria, Norway, Italy and Spain before coming to England.

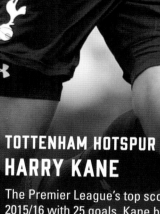

TOTTENHAM HOTSPUR
HARRY KANE

The Premier League's top scorer in 2015/16 with 25 goals, Kane bagged 21 the year before (31 in all competitions). Now 23, Harry debuted for Tottenham in 2011 in a Europa League game with Hearts before loans with Leyton Orient, Millwall, Norwich and Leicester helped him develop his game. Now one of the most feared strikers in the league Kane started the season with five goals in 16 games for England.

WEST HAM UNITED
SIMONE ZAZA

Italy international Simone Zaza is on a year's loan to the Hammers who have the option of signing the 25-year-old from Juventus for a fee that would total over 20m Euros. Although infamous for his flamboyantly fluffed penalty against Germany at Euro 2016, Zaza is a real dangerman because as well as offering pace and strength he is also a threat in the air.

SKILLS: THE RAINBOW KICK

1 Start off with your feet on either side of the ball

2 Use one foot to roll the ball up your other leg

Make sure to roll the ball hard enough to give it some air

3

4 When the ball is in the air strike it with your heel

5 ...and flick it over your head!

Brazilian star striker, Neymar, is well known for his use of the rainbow kick on the pitch and regularly fools his opposition. The trick is an impressive show of skill which takes practise, practise practise!

TIP: Lean forward as you're doing the tric this helps create space between you and the ball so you can strike it more easi

CRYSTAL PALACE F.C.

SCOTT
6 DANN

Can you figure out the identity of these Eagles stars?

CRYSTAL PALACE F.C.

A

B

E

WHO ARE YA?

ANSWERS ON PAGE 6

C

D

CRYSTAL PALACE F.C.
1905

F

G

EURO 2016

Six Eagles represented their countries at the summer's European Championships in France, with all of the clubs' star international players reaching the knockout stages of the tournament

Back in June, Jonny Williams and Joe Ledley featured in Wales' opening match of the tournament against Slovakia which brought a 2-1 win, with Wayne Hennessey missing that game with a slight back complaint. He started alongside Ledley for the remainder of their matches throughout the competition, with Williams also handed caps in the defeat against England and the last 16 win against Northern Ireland.

Chris Coleman's team came up against Belgium in the quarter-finals, whom Christian Benteke had played twice for as a substitute during the group stages, but Wales ran out 3-1 winners to continue their march to glory, before their ultimate exit at the hands of Portugal in the semi-final, where all three Welsh Eagles featured.

By that stage, only Bayern Munich boasted more players still at the tournament than the Eagles, with Williams, Ledley and Hennessey joined in the final four by hosts France, who boasted Yohan Cabaye and new signing Steve Mandanda in their ranks.

While Mandanda saw no action during the competition as backup to team captain Hugo Lloris, Cabaye played the full 90 minutes during Les Bleus' 0-0 draw with Switzerland in their final group game in his home town of Lille and came on for the final seconds of Didier Deschamps' side's semi-final success against Germany. However the Palace man was forced to watch the whole of the final from the bench as Portugal clinched their first international championship thanks to an extra-time strike from Eder.

CHRISTIAN
BENTEKE
17

Andy Johnson was named Player of the Year...

The Eagles beat the Hammers 1-0 in the Play-Off final

...and top-scored with 32 in all competitions

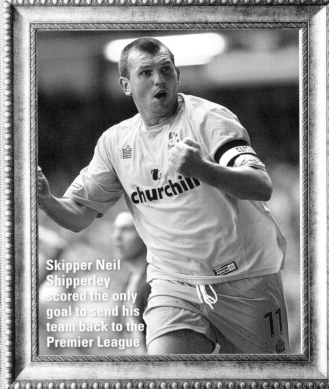

Skipper Neil Shipperley scored the only goal to send his team back to the Premier League

The season finished with former Palace striker Iain Dowie as manager

SPOT THE SEASON

N West Ham United's captain

O Leicester's manager when they last won the League Cup in 2000

P West Bromwich Albion's first summer signing

Q

R The manager who led the Foxes to the Premier League title

S Captain of Stoke City

Signed for Sunderland a striker a later beca the club' chairma

The answer to each clue begins with the corresponding letter of the alphabe

T

U

Tottenham Hotspur's kit manufacturer

werton's ckname

V

Stoke City played their home games here before moving to the Britannia Stadium

W

Southampton's anthem

X

Arsenal's first summer signing

Y

Liverpool's club motto

Z

Chelsea's player of the year in 2003

DESIGN
YOUR OWN
FOOTIE
BOOTS

JASON
PUNCHEON
42

There are five Premier League managers hidden in the crowd

CRYSTAL PALACE F.C.

ANSWERS ON PAGE 6

SPOT THE BOSS

WILFRIED ZAHA

PLAYER OF THE YEAR

Once again a series of electrifying displays on the right flank for the Eagles saw the academy graduate scoop the club's Player of the Year award for the first time in his career.

A high level of consistent displays ensured Zaha remained a regular in the team despite the arrivals of Chung-yong Lee and Bakary Sako, but even with competition for a wide midfield berth as intense as ever going into 2015/16, the Croydon native missed just four matches in all competitions over the course of the campaign.

Things started well for Zaha when he scored Palace's first goal of the season in acrobatic style against Norwich City on the opening day, and his quick feet and dazzling skills were soon being put to good use on a regular basis, and in late September he repeated his 2013 Championship play-off heroics to win a penalty against Watford which Yohan Cabaye converted to give the Eagles a big early season win.

After also scoring in the 5-1 romp against Newcastle United in November, Zaha helped pave the way for the Eagles' run to the FA Cup final by netting winning goals against Southampton and Stoke City in the early rounds, and has played every minute available in the competition so far, leading him to a final appearance against his former club Manchester United at Wembley which saw Palace come so close to clinching their first major piece of silverware.

He has also been a frequent provider of goals for Alan Pardew's men, and easily surpassed his previous best of three Premier League assists which came in 2014/15. January 2016 also brought up another big milestone for the 23-year-old when he played in his 200th game for the club during his two spells with the Eagles.

Can you spot the season from these five clues?

Jubilant goalkeeper John Burridge

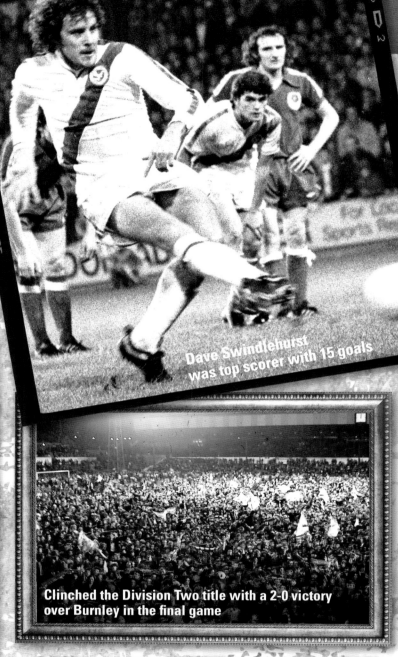

Dave Swindlehurst was top scorer with 15 goals

The Boss, Terry Venables

Clinched the Division Two title with a 2-0 victory over Burnley in the final game

SPOT THE SEASON

Player of the Year, Kenny Sansom

ANSWER ON PAGE 62

WILFRIED
ZAHA
11

There's very little to put a smile on a striker's face more than scoring a hat-trick in a winning performance.

Take a look back at three special Eagles' trebles...

HAT-TRICK

IAN WRIGHT V WIMBLEDON
SATURDAY 4 MAY 1991

Under the management of Steve Coppell, Palace completed their final away fixture of the 1990/91 season on a real high note as star striker Ian Wright scored all three goals in a 3-0 triumph at Plough Lane.

Wright opened the scoring with a crisp low finish and then came one of the striker's greatest ever Palace goals. He collected the ball just inside the Wimbledon half and hit a sublime lob that dipped over stranded Dons 'keeper Hans Segers from all of 40 yards. The third goal was an angled finish from close range and became Palace's first hat-trick away from Selhurst Park since 1963.

Palace wrapped up the season with a 3-0 home victory over Manchester United to seal a highest ever top-flight finish of third in the old First Division.

ANDY JOHNSON V BRIGHTON & HA
SATURDAY 26 OCTOBER 2002

Diminutive striker Andy Johnson certainly won over the Selhurst Park faithful following his move from Birmingham City by netting a memorable Nationwide First Division hat-trick against arch-rivals Brighton & Hove Albion in October 2002.

Johnson got the home side off to the best possible start when he opened the scoring after just four minutes. He headed home his second goal of the game after 35 minutes to give Palace a two-goal cushion at the break.

Dougie Freedman extended the lead six minutes into the second half before AJ completed his hat-trick by winning and scoring a penalty. Julian Gray completed the rout with Palace's fifth goal on a memorable afternoon at Selhurst Park.

HEROES

DANNY BUTTERFIELD V WOLVES
TUESDAY, FEBRUARY 2, 2010

Right-back Danny Butterfield played over 250 games for Crystal Palace and is one of the club's more unlikely hat-trick heroes. However, his exploits against in an FA Cup Fourth Round replay in 2010 saw him score the fastest hat-trick in the club's history.

After the two sides had played out an entertaining 2-2 draw at Molineux, few would have expected Butterfield to be the man to seal Palace's place in the fifth round and a tie against Aston Villa.

On a memorable night for Butterfield, under the Selhurst Park floodlights, he netted the perfect hat-trick with a goal from either foot plus a header and all in the space of seven second-half minutes! A late Karl Henry goal saw Palace run-out 4-1 winners.

SKILLS: THE MARADONA SPIN

1
Start off by simply dribbling the ball

2
While moving in a forward motion, tap the ball with your leading foot...

3
...and start turning your body in the opposite direction

4
As you're spinning, pull the ball back with your other foot while continuing to turn

5

6
Then keep moving forward!

Argentinian maestro, Maradona, is very well known for this move. It is brilliant for overcoming opponents and getting yourself into space, as while you are spinning you are putting your back to the defender and shielding the ball.

CLUB OR COUNTRY

Can you work out which Premier League club, Championship club or country each set of clues is pointing to...

1.

2.

4.

5.

6.

8.

9.

ANSWERS ON PAGE 62

FIVE GAMES TO LOOK FOR IN THE SECOND HALF OF THE SEASON

The second-half of the 2016/17 season certainly looks like being a thrilling ride for all Eagles fans. We take a look at five key fixtures scheduled in the calendar year of 2017.

2ND HALF

FIRST TRIP TO THE LONDON STADIUM

London derby matches with West Ham United have a tendency to be entertaining affairs and Alan Pardew facing one of his former teams always adds to the occasion. However, our meeting with the Hammers on Saturday, January 14 will take on a historic feel as we make a first-ever visit to the London Stadium.

The former Olympic Stadium became the Hammers' new 60,000 capacity home at the start of this season and under the management of Slaven Bilic the move is anticipated to herald an exciting new era for the club. This match is sure to be a real cracker!

SPURS AT SELHURST

After suffering a league double at the hands of London rivals Tottenham Hotspur last season, Palace will certainly be looking to set the record straight when they come face-to-face with Mauricio Pochettino's talented troops on Saturday, March 11.

Spurs produced a second-half master-class at Selhurst Park last season as they attempted to rein in league leaders Leicester City. Despite trailing at the break after a Jan Vertonghen own goal had given the Eagles a 1-0 lead, the visitors stormed back after the interval to win 3-1 with goals from Harry Kane, Dele Alli and Nacer Chadli.

ENTERTAINING ARSENAL

Arsenal provided the opposition for the Eagles' first home game last season but this time around the Selhurst Park faithful will have to wait until Saturday, April 8 to see us lock horns with Arsene Wenger's men on home soil.

Last season's 2-1 reverse was harsh on the Eagles and the team showed they were more than a match for the Gunners when a Yannick Bolasie goal secured a 1-1 draw at the Emirates later in the campaign. Once again, with capital pride at stake this promises to be yet another must-see match at Selhurst Park.

CHAMPIONS IN TOWN

There is nothing better than testing yourself against the best. And the best of the bunch last season were surprise package Leicester City who will visit Selhurst Park as Premier League champions on Saturday, April 15.

The Foxes recorded a league double over Palace last season with two 1-0 triumphs en route to the title. Sandwiched in between Arsenal at home and Liverpool away this is sure to be another tough assignment on home soil.

ENDING AT OLD TRAFFORD

In a repeat of last season's FA Cup Final, Palace will once again complete their campaign with a meeting with Manchester United when they wrap up their 2016/17 Premier League fixtures by facing Jose Mourinho's men at Old Trafford on Sunday, May 21.

As always, a trip to the Theatre of Dreams is never an easy task and a lot is expected of United under Mourinho this season - so much so many feel Palace could be gate crashing and an end-of-season party if all goes according to plan for Zlatan Ibrahimovic and co.

JANUARY 2017

Mon 2	Swansea City	H	3.00pm
Sat 14	West Ham United	A	3.00pm
Sat 21	Everton	H	3.00pm
Tue 31	Bournemouth	A	7.45pm

FEBRUARY 2017

Sat 4	Sunderland	H	3.00pm
Sat 11	Stoke City	A	3.00pm
Sat 25	Middlesbrough	H	3.00pm

MARCH 2017

Sat 4	West Bromwich Albion	A	3.00pm
Sat 11	Tottenham Hotspur	H	3.00pm
Sat 18	Watford	H	3.00pm

APRIL 2017

Sat 1	Chelsea	A	3.00pm
Wed 5	Southampton	A	7.45pm
Sat 8	Arsenal	H	3.00pm
Sat 15	Leicester City	H	3.00pm
Sat 22	Liverpool	A	3.00pm
Sat 29	Burnley	H	3.00pm

MAY 2017

Sat 6	Manchester City	A	3.00pm
Sat 13	Hull City	H	3.00pm
Sun 21	Manchester Utd	A	3.00pm

A

B

There are too many footballs! Work out which is the real ball in each photo.

ANSWERS ON PAGE

CHUNG-YONG
14 LEE

What do you think will happen in 2017?

2016/17

PREMIER LEAGUE

PREDICTION FOR CHAMPIONSHIP WINNERS:
Norwich City

YOUR PREDICTION:

PREDICTION FOR ALSO PROMOTED TO THE PREMIER LEAGUE:
Derby County & Birmingham City

YOUR PREDICTION:

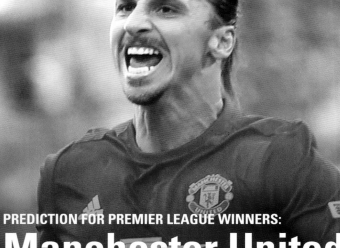

PREDICTION FOR PREMIER LEAGUE WINNERS:
Manchester United

YOUR PREDICTION:

PREDICTION FOR PREMIER LEAGUE RUNNERS-UP:
Chelsea

YOUR PREDICTION:

THE CHAMPIONSHIP

PREDICTIONS

THE FA CUP

PREDICTION FOR FA CUP WINNERS:
Crystal Palace

YOUR PREDICTION:

PREDICTION FOR FA CUP FINALISTS:
Liverpool

YOUR PREDICTION:

PREDICTION FOR LEAGUE CUP WINNERS:
Arsenal

YOUR PREDICTION:

PREDICTION FOR LEAGUE CUP FINALISTS:
Manchester City

YOUR PREDICTION:

THE LEAGUE CUP

ANSWERS

PAGE 19 – SPOT THE SEASON
1989/90.

PAGE 22 – SPOT THE DIFFERENCE

PAGE 26 – A–Z OF THE PREMIER LEAGUE
A. Tony Adams. B. Boothferry Park. C. Jim Cannon.
D. Nathan Dyer. E. Michael Essien. F. Marc-Vivien Foe
G. Andre Gray. H. Eddie Howe. I. In pursuit of excellence
J. Sir Elton John. K. Vincent Kompany. L. Jesse Lingard
M. Steve McClaren.

PAGE 31 – ON THE ROAD
Arsenal - Emirates Stadium. Bournemouth - Vitality
Stadium. Burnley - Turf Moor. Chelsea - Stamford Bridge.
Crystal Palace - Selhurst Park. Everton - Goodison Park.
Hull - KC Stadium. Leicester - King Power Stadium.
Liverpool - Anfield. Man City - Etihad Stadium.
Man United - Old Trafford. Middlesbrough - Riverside
Stadium. Southampton - St Mary's Stadium.
Stoke - bet365 Stadium. Sunderland - Stadium of Light.
Swansea - Liberty Stadium. Tottenham - White Hart Lane.
Watford - Vicarage Road. West Brom - The Hawthorns.
West Ham - London Stadium.

PAGE 38 – WHO ARE YA?
A. Joe Ledley. B. Jason Puncheon. C. Connor Wickham.
D. Wayne Hennessey. E. Mathieu Flamini. F. Joel Ward.
G. Jonathan Benteke.

PAGE 43 – SPOT THE SEASON
2003/04.

PAGE 44 – A–Z OF THE PREMIER LEAGUE
N. Mark Noble. O. Martin O'Neill. P. Matt Phillips.
Q. Niall Quinn. R. Claudio Ranieri. S. Ryan Shawcross.
T. The Toffees. U. Under Armour. V. Victoria Ground.
W. When the Saints go marching in. X. Granit Xhaka.
Y. You'll never walk alone. Z. Gianfranco Zola.

PAGE 48 – SPOT THE BOSS
David Moyes, Eddie Howe, Jose Mourinho,
Pep Guardiola and Arsene Wenger.

PAGE 51 – SPOT THE SEASON
1978/79.

PAGE 55 – CLUB OR COUNTRY
1. Hull City. 2. Newcastle United. 3. Spain. 4. Austria.
5. Wigan Athletic. 6. Tottenham Hotspur. 7. Iceland.
8. Arsenal. 9. Wolverhampton Wanderers.

PAGE 58 – WHAT BALL?
Picture A - Ball 3. Picture B - Ball 2.